MIAMI DOLPHINS

BY JOSH ANDERSON

Stride
An Imprint of The Child's World®
childsworld.com

The Child's World
childsworld.com

Published by The Child's World®
800-599-READ • www.childsworld.com

Photography Credits
Cover: © Elsa / Staff / Getty Images; page 1: © Africa Studio / Shutterstock; page 3: © Rob Carr / Staff / Getty Images; page 5: © Eric Espada / Stringer / Getty Images; page 6: © The Palm Beach Post/ZUMA Press / Newscom; page 9: © Mark Brown / Stringer / Getty Images; page 10: © Michael Reaves / Stringer / Getty Images; page 11: © stevezmina1 / Getty Images; page 12: © Michael Reaves / Stringer / Getty Images; page 12: © Jonathan Daniel / Staff / Getty Images; page 13: © MIKE JULA / "Ai Wire Photo Service" / Newscom; page 13: © John Grieshop / Stringer / Getty Images; page 14: © Michael Reaves / Stringer / Getty Images; page 15: © Mark Trowbridge / Staff / Getty Images; page 16: © Cliff Welch/Icon SMI / Newscom; page 16: © Tony Tomsic / SportsChrome / Newscom; page 17: © Andy Lyons / Staff / Getty Images; page 17: © Paul Warfield / Associated Press; page 18: © ASSOCIATED PRESS / Associated Press; page 18: © Tony Tomsic / SportsChrome / Newscom; page 19: © Icon SMI / Newscom; page 19: © Al Bello / Staff / Getty Images; page 20: © Michael Reaves / Stringer / Getty Images; page 20: © David Eulitt / Stringer / Getty Images; page 21: © Harry How / Staff / Getty Images; page 21: © Michael Reaves / Stringer / Getty Images; page 22: © Ai Wire Photo Service / Newscom; page 23: © Streeter Lecka / Staff / Getty Images; page 23: © stevezmina1 / Getty Images; page 25: © John Walthe/TNS / Newscom; page 26: © David Bergman/TNS / Newscom; page 29: © Stephen Dunn / Staff / Getty Images

ISBN Information
9781503857674 (Reinforced Library Binding)
9781503860568 (Portable Document Format)
9781503861923 (Online Multi-user eBook)
9781503863286 (Electronic Publication)

LCCN 2021952633

Printed in the United States of America

BRINGING THE WORLD TO YOUNG READERS 1968

TABLE OF CONTENTS

GO DOLPHINS!

The Miami Dolphins compete in the National Football **League's** (NFL's) American Football Conference (AFC). They play in the AFC East **division**, along with the Buffalo Bills, New England Patriots, and New York Jets. In 1972, Dolphins fans witnessed something truly historic. The team went undefeated in the regular season and postseason. It was the only perfect season in NFL history, and fans still celebrate it today. Let's learn more about the Dolphins!

AFC EAST DIVISION

Buffalo Bills

Miami Dolphins

New England Patriots

New York Jets

TIGHT END MIKE GESICKI (LEFT) IS MORE THAN 6 FEET (183 CM) TALL. THAT MAKES HIM A DANGEROUS TARGET IN THE END ZONE.

100
PATRIOTS

BECOMING THE DOLPHINS

The Dolphins joined the American Football League (AFL) as an **expansion team** in 1966. Team owners held a name-the-team contest for fans. Team owner Joe Robbie said he chose "Dolphins" because they're one of the fastest and smartest creatures in the sea. The team joined the NFL when the AFL and NFL combined in 1970. From 1971 to 1973, the Dolphins played in three-straight **Super Bowls**, winning two of them.

DON SHULA (LEFT) COACHED THE DOLPHINS FOR 26 SEASONS, AND JOE ROBBIE (RIGHT) WAS THE TEAM'S FIRST OWNER.

BY THE NUMBERS

The Dolphins have played in **FIVE** Super Bowls.

14
division titles for the Dolphins

513
points scored by the team in 1984—a Dolphins record!

TEN
Dolphins enshrined in the Pro Football **Hall of Fame**

QUARTERBACK RYAN FITZPATRICK (TOP) EARNED THE NICKNAME "FITZMAGIC" FOR HIS ABILITY TO LEAD HIS TEAMS TO LATE-GAME VICTORIES.

DOLPHINS PLAYERS AND STAFF ENTER HARD ROCK STADIUM THROUGH A GIANT TUNNEL SHAPED LIKE THE SUN, A POPULAR SIGHT IN MIAMI.

GAME DAY

Since 1987, the Dolphins have played their home games at Hard Rock **Stadium**. From 1993 until 2011, the team shared the stadium with the Miami Marlins, a Major League Baseball team. Now the Marlins play in nearby loanDepot Park. On game days, Hard Rock Stadium holds about 65,000 fans. Six Super Bowls have been played there. Miami is one of the warmest cities to host an NFL team. Average temperatures during certain parts of the season are higher than 80 degrees Fahrenheit (27 degrees Celsius).

We're Famous!

The plot of the 1994 movie *Ace Ventura: Pet Detective* features the Dolphins. In the film, the Dolphins mascot, a real bottlenose dolphin, is stolen. Ace Ventura, played by comedian Jim Carrey, is hired to find the creature. Legendary Dolphins quarterback Dan Marino had a part in the film too!

UNIFORM

AQUA

WHITE

Truly Weird

In 1980, an NBC sports producer decided to try something different for the television broadcast of a game between the Dolphins and New York Jets. No announcers described the action on the field. The only sounds viewers heard were those coming straight from the stadium itself. The experiment was considered a failure and hasn't been tried since. The Dolphins lost the game 24–17.

Alternate Jersey

Sometimes teams wear an alternate jersey that is different from their home and away jerseys. It might be a bright color or have a unique theme. In 2016, the Dolphins wore all-orange uniforms for a game against the Cincinnati Bengals. The new look proved unlucky—the Dolphins lost 22–7.

DOLPHINS FANS FIND CREATIVE WAYS TO CHEER FOR THEIR TEAM DURING HOME GAMES AT HARD ROCK STADIUM.

TEAM SPIRIT

Going to a game at Hard Rock Stadium can be loads of fun! Every time the team scores a **touchdown**, fans sing the team fight song, "Miami Dolphins Number One." And if you see fans holding a hand straight up on their foreheads, they're giving you a "Fins Up" salute!

From 1966 until 1968, a real dolphin named Flipper swam in a tank inside the team's original stadium. Nowadays, the Miami Dolphins Cheerleaders are joined at the games by T. D., the team's costumed dolphin mascot. T. D. stands for "The Dolphin."

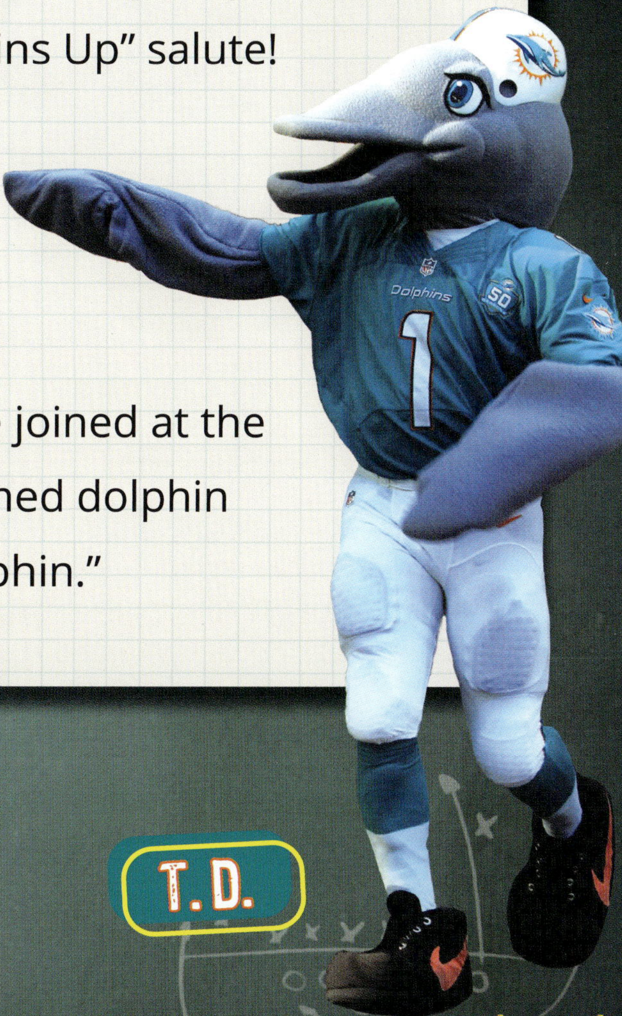

T. D.

HEROES OF HISTORY

Larry Csonka

Running Back | 1968–1974, 1979

Hall-of-Famer Csonka's powerful running helped led the Dolphins to two championship seasons. He won the **Most Valuable Player** (MVP) Award after Super Bowl 8 when he rushed for 145 yards and two touchdowns. Csonka's 6,737 rushing yards with the team are the most in Dolphins history.

Bob Griese

Quarterback | 1967–1980

Griese's 25,092 passing yards and 192 passing touchdowns both rank second in team history. He was chosen for eight Pro Bowls and led the Dolphins to three AFC Championships. He was inducted to the Pro Football Hall of Fame in 1990.

Jason Taylor

Defensive End | 1997–2007, 2009, 2011

Taylor ranks seventh all-time with 139.5 **sacks**. He forced nine fumbles in 2006—one shy of the NFL record. Taylor was selected for six Pro Bowls. In 2017, he was inducted into the Pro Football Hall of Fame.

Paul Warfield

Wide Receiver | 1970–1974

Hall-of-Famer Warfield was the top receiver on the Dolphins' two Super Bowl winning teams in 1972 and 1973. He was chosen for the Pro Bowl in each of his five seasons with the Dolphins. Warfield led the NFL with 11 touchdown catches in 1971.

The Dolphins defeat the Kansas City Chiefs 27–24 in a two **overtime** playoff game. It's the longest game in NFL history.

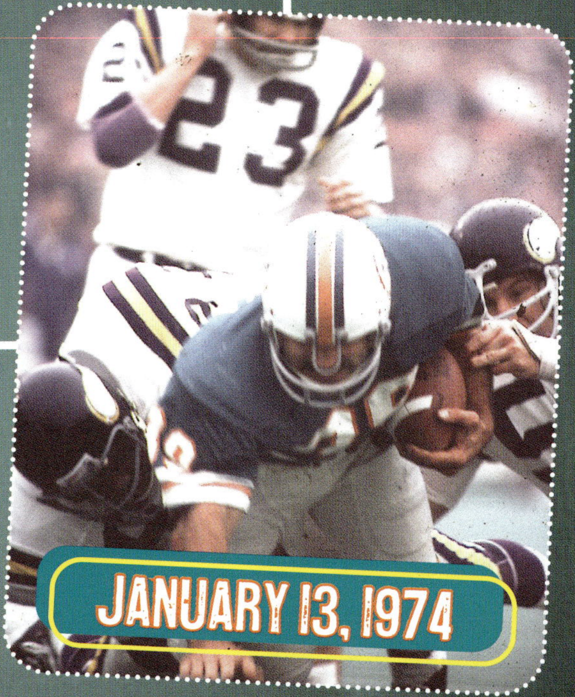

The Dolphins defeat the Minnesota Vikings 24–7 in Super Bowl 8. It's their second Super Bowl victory in a row!

BIG DAYS

JANUARY 6, 1985

Dan Marino leads the Dolphins past the Steelers 45–28 in the AFC Championship Game. They earn a trip to the Super Bowl.

DECEMBER 28, 2008

A victory over the New York Jets clinches the Dolphins' first AFC East division title since 2000.

MODERN-DAY MARVELS

Tyreek Hill

Wide Receiver | Debut: 2022

Hill played his first six seasons for the Kansas City Chiefs. He was traded to the Dolphins before the 2022 season. Hill has been selected for the Pro Bowl in each of his first six seasons. He reached 4,000 yards receiving for his career in only 58 games. Hill is shown here in his old Chiefs uniform.

Xavien Howard

Cornerback | Debut: 2016

Howard's 22 interceptions from 2017 to 2020 were the most in the NFL during that time. He was chosen for the Pro Bowl after the 2018, 2020, and 2021 seasons. His ten interceptions in 2020 led the NFL, and his seven in 2018 were tied for the most in the league.

Tua Tagovailoa

Quarterback | Debut: 2020

The Dolphins selected Tagovailoa with the fifth overall pick in the 2020 NFL Draft. He became the starting quarterback a few games into the 2020 season. As a **rookie**, Tagovailoa threw 11 touchdowns and only five interceptions. In the 2021 season, he led the Dolphins to a 7–5 record.

Jaylen Waddle

Wide Receiver | Debut: 2021

The Dolphins chose Waddle with the sixth pick in the 2021 NFL Draft. He had nearly 2,000 yards receiving during three seasons at the University of Alabama. Waddle caught 104 passes in 2021. That's more catches than any rookie in NFL history!

Many consider Dan Marino to be one of the greatest quarterbacks ever to play in the NFL.

THE GOAT

GREATEST OF ALL TIME

DAN MARINO

After retiring as the all-time leader in both categories, Marino currently ranks seventh with 61,361 passing yards and 420 passing touchdowns. In 1984, he won the MVP Award and led the Dolphins to the Super Bowl. Overall, he led the Dolphins to the **playoffs** ten different times. Also in 1984, Marino became the first player ever to throw for more than 5,000 yards in a season. He was selected for the **Pro Bowl** nine times. After retiring, Marino was enshrined in the Pro Football Hall of Fame in 2005.

FAN FAVORITE

Ricky Williams–Running Back
2002–2003, 2005, 2007–2010

After three seasons with the New Orleans Saints, Williams rushed into the hearts of Dolphins fans with one of the greatest seasons ever. In 2002, he rushed for 1,853 yards and 16 touchdowns. Although he never reached those heights again, he'll always be a cherished part of Dolphins history.

THE BIG GAME

JANUARY 14, 1973 – SUPER BOWL 7

The Dolphins finished the 1972 regular season with a perfect 14–0 record. They defeated the Cleveland Browns and Pittsburgh Steelers in playoff games to earn a trip to Super Bowl 7. Their opponent was the Washington Redskins, now known as the Washington Football Team. If the Dolphins could win, they'd become the only team to finish a season as champions with no losses or ties. Miami scored touchdowns in each of the first two quarters but failed to score again. Washington only managed one touchdown during the entire game. The Dolphins won 14–7 and became the only team in NFL history to complete a perfect season.

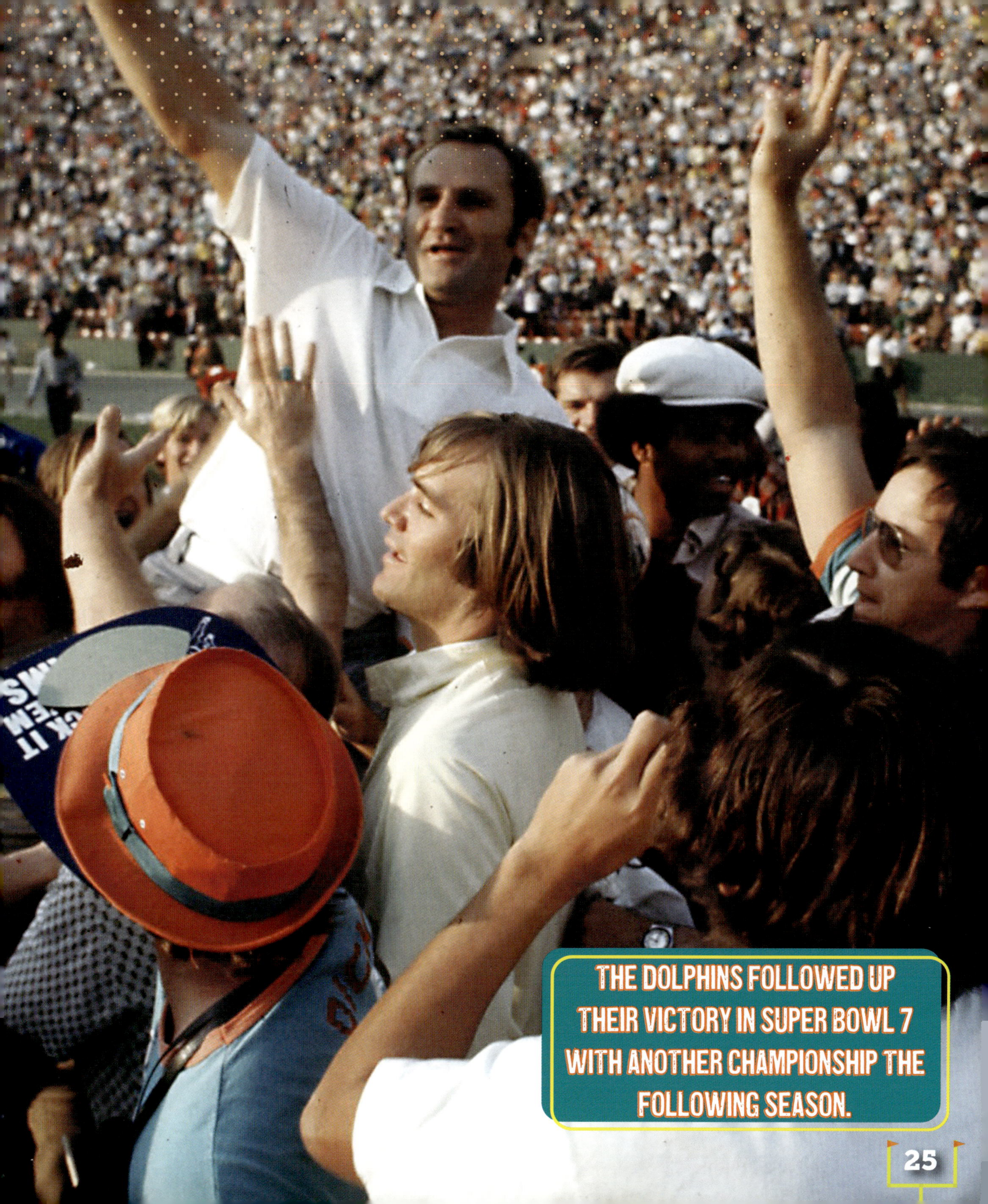

THE DOLPHINS FOLLOWED UP THEIR VICTORY IN SUPER BOWL 7 WITH ANOTHER CHAMPIONSHIP THE FOLLOWING SEASON.

DON SHULA'S 328 COACHING VICTORIES ARE THE MOST IN NFL HISTORY. HE EARNED 257 OF THOSE WITH THE DOLPHINS.

AMAZING FEATS

4,208 Passing Yards

In 2015 by QUARTERBACK Ryan Tannehill

15 Rushing Touchdowns

In 1997 by RUNNING BACK Abdul-Karim al-Jabbar

18 Receiving Touchdowns

In 1984 for WIDE RECEIVER Mark Clayton

1,313 Receiving Yards

In 1986 for WIDE RECEIVER Mark Duper

ALL-TIME BEST

PASSING YARDS

Dan Marino
61,361
Bob Griese
25,092
Ryan Tannehill
20,434

RUSHING YARDS

Larry Csonka
6,737
Ricky Williams
6,436
Ronnie Brown
4,815

RECEIVING YARDS

Mark Duper
8,869
Mark Clayton
8,643
Nat Moore
7,546

SACKS*

Jason Taylor
131
Cameron Wake
98
Bill Stanfill
69.5

SCORING

Olindo Mare
1,048
Garo Yepremian
830
Pete Stoyanovich
774

INTERCEPTIONS

Jake Scott
35
Dick Anderson
34
Sam Madison
31

*unofficial before 1982

WIDE RECEIVER MARK DUPER PLAYED ALL 11 OF HIS NFL SEASONS WITH THE DOLPHINS.

GLOSSARY

division (dih-VIZSH-un): a group of teams within the NFL that play each other more frequently and compete for the best record

expansion team (ek-SPAN-shun TEEM): a new team added to the league

Hall of Fame (HAHL of FAYM): a museum in Canton, Ohio, that honors the best players in NFL history

league (LEEG): an organization of sports teams that compete against each other

Most Valuable Player (MOHST VAL-yuh-bul PLAY-uhr): a yearly award given to the top player in the NFL

overtime (OH-vuhr-tym): extra time played when teams are tied at the end of four quarters

playoffs (PLAY-ahfs): a series of games played after the regular season that decides which two teams play in the Super Bowl

Pro Bowl (PRO BOWL): the NFL's All-Star game where the best players in the league compete

rookie (RUH-kee): a player playing in his first season

sack (SAK): when a quarterback is tackled behind the line of scrimmage before he can throw the ball

stadium (STAY-dee-uhm): a building with a field and seats for fans where teams play

Super Bowl (SOO-puhr BOWL): the championship game of the NFL, played between the winners of the AFC and the NFC

touchdown (TUTCH-down): a play in which the ball is brought into the other team's end zone, resulting in six points

FIND OUT MORE

IN THE LIBRARY

Bulgar, Beth and Mark Bechtel. *My First Book of Football.* New York, NY: Time Inc. Books, 2015.

Jacobs, Greg. *The Everything Kids' Football Book, 7th Edition*. Avon, MA: Adams Media, 2021.

Sports Illustrated Kids. *The Greatest Football Teams of All Time*. New York, NY: Time Inc. Books, 2018.

Wyner, Zach. *Miami Dolphins*. New York, NY: AV2 Books, 2020.

ON THE WEB

Visit our website for links about the Miami Dolphins:
childsworld.com/links

Note to parents, teachers, and librarians: We routinely verify our web links to make sure they are safe and active sites. Encourage your readers to check them out!

INDEX

ABOUT THE AUTHOR

Josh Anderson has published over 50 books for children and young adults. His two boys are the greatest joys in his life. Hobbies include coaching his sons in youth basketball, no-holds-barred games of Apples to Apples, and taking long family walks. His favorite NFL team is a secret he'll never share!